First World War
and Army of Occupation
War Diary
France, Belgium and Germany

3 CAVALRY DIVISION
6 Cavalry Brigade
10th (Prince of Wales' Own Royal) Hussars
1 March 1918 - 31 March 1919

WO95/1153/3

The Naval & Military Press Ltd
www.nmarchive.com
Published in association with The National Archives

Published by

The Naval & Military Press Ltd

Unit 10 Ridgewood Industrial Park,

Uckfield, East Sussex,

TN22 5QE England

Tel: +44 (0) 1825 749494

www.naval-military-press.com

www.nmarchive.com

This diary has been reprinted in facsimile from the original. Any imperfections are inevitably reproduced and the quality may fall short of modern type and cartographic standards.

© **Crown Copyright**
Images reproduced by permission of The National Archives, London, England, 2015.

Contents

Document type	Place/Title	Date From	Date To
Heading	WO95/1153/3 3 Cavalry Division 6 Cavalry Bridge 10 (prince of wales) Hussars Mar 1918, Mar 1919.		
Heading	1914 1918-19 3rd Cavalry Division 6th Cavalry Brigade.10th Hussars Mar 1918-Mar 1919 From 8 Bde 3 Cav Div Box 1156 To Hussars Bde Box 1166		
War Diary	Tertry	01/03/1918	13/03/1918
War Diary	Devise	14/03/1918	21/03/1918
War Diary	Beaumont	22/03/1918	22/03/1918
War Diary	Pontoise	23/03/1918	23/03/1918
War Diary	Carlepont	24/03/1918	26/03/1918
War Diary	Choisy	27/03/1918	29/03/1918
War Diary	Airion	30/03/1918	30/03/1918
War Diary	Sains-En-Amienois	31/03/1918	31/03/1918
War Diary	Pontoise	23/03/1918	23/03/1918
War Diary	Berlancourt	24/03/1918	24/03/1918
War Diary	Guiscard	25/03/1918	25/03/1918
War Diary	Lagny	26/03/1918	26/03/1918
War Diary	Elincourt	27/03/1918	27/03/1918
War Diary	Chevincourt	28/03/1918	29/03/1918
War Diary	Viry Naureuil	22/03/1918	22/03/1918
War Diary	Noureuil	23/03/1918	24/03/1918
War Diary	Abbecourt	25/03/1918	25/03/1918
War Diary	Les Bruyers	26/03/1918	26/03/1918
Heading	6th Cav. Bde. 3rd Cav. Div. War Diary 10th (Prince Of Wales's Own Royal) Hussars. April 1918		
War Diary	Racineuse Farm	01/04/1918	01/04/1918
War Diary	Gentelles Wood	02/04/1918	02/04/1918
War Diary	Fouilloy	03/04/1918	05/04/1918
War Diary	Blangy Tronville	06/04/1918	06/04/1918
War Diary	Camon	07/04/1918	11/04/1918
War Diary	Buire-Au-Bois	12/04/1918	12/04/1918
War Diary	Hestrus	13/04/1918	13/04/1918
War Diary	Aumerval	10/04/1918	04/05/1918
War Diary	Rougefay	05/05/1918	05/05/1918
War Diary	Villers L'Hopital	06/05/1918	06/05/1918
War Diary	Contay	07/05/1918	17/05/1918
War Diary	Belloy-Sur-Somme	18/05/1918	31/05/1918
War Diary	Behencourt	01/06/1918	14/06/1918
War Diary	Belloy-Sur-Somme	15/06/1918	25/06/1918
War Diary	Reincourt	26/06/1918	06/08/1918
War Diary	Renancourt	07/08/1918	09/08/1918
War Diary	Caix	10/08/1918	10/08/1918
War Diary	Folies	11/08/1918	11/08/1918
War Diary	Fouencamps	12/08/1918	15/08/1918
War Diary	Riencourt	16/08/1918	21/08/1918
War Diary	Fieffes	22/08/1918	25/08/1918
War Diary	Vitz Villeroy	26/08/1918	28/08/1918
War Diary	Sibiville	29/08/1918	30/08/1918
War Diary	Wailly	31/08/1918	01/09/1918
War Diary	Wancourt	02/09/1918	02/09/1918

War Diary	Wailly	03/09/1918	05/09/1918
War Diary	Sibiville	06/09/1918	06/09/1918
War Diary	Vieil Hesdin	07/09/1918	16/09/1918
War Diary	Grigny	17/09/1918	17/09/1918
War Diary	Boisbergues	18/09/1918	18/09/1918
War Diary	Vieil Hesdin	19/09/1918	19/09/1918
War Diary	Ligny-sur-Canche	20/09/1918	26/09/1918
War Diary	Meaute	27/09/1918	27/09/1918
War Diary	Hem	28/09/1918	30/09/1918
War Diary	Bihecourt	01/10/1918	03/10/1918
War Diary	Pontru	04/10/1918	05/10/1918
War Diary	Trefcon	06/10/1918	08/10/1918
War Diary	Ligny Le Fosse	09/10/1918	09/10/1918
War Diary	Reumont	10/10/1918	10/10/1918
War Diary	Montigny	11/10/1918	11/10/1918
War Diary	Elincourt	12/10/1918	13/10/1918
War Diary	Banteux	14/10/1918	14/10/1918
War Diary	Manancourt	15/10/1918	06/11/1918
War Diary	Marquion	07/11/1918	07/11/1918
War Diary	Esquerchin	08/11/1918	08/11/1918
War Diary	Fretin	09/11/1918	10/11/1918
War Diary	Gourain	11/11/1918	11/11/1918
War Diary	Willaupuis	12/11/1918	16/11/1918
War Diary	St. Marcoule	17/11/1918	17/11/1918
War Diary	Saintes	18/11/1918	20/11/1918
War Diary	Limal	21/11/1918	21/11/1918
War Diary	Taviers	22/11/1918	23/11/1918
War Diary	St. Germain	24/11/1918	09/12/1918
War Diary	Moha	10/12/1918	11/12/1918
War Diary	Seraing-Le-Chateau	12/12/1918	28/02/1919
Heading	War Diary of 10th Hussars March 1919		
War Diary	Seraing Le Chateau	01/03/1919	14/03/1919
War Diary	Sprimont	15/03/1919	17/03/1919
War Diary	Theux	18/03/1919	18/03/1919
War Diary	Raeren	19/03/1919	19/03/1919
War Diary	Hongen	20/03/1919	20/03/1919
War Diary	Konigshoven	21/03/1919	31/03/1919

(3)

WO 95/1153

3 Cavalry Division
6 Cavalry Brigade

10 (Prince of Wales) Hussars

Mar 1918 - Mar 1919.

1914. 1918-19
3RD CAVALRY DIVISION
6TH CAVALRY BRIGADE.

10TH HUSSARS.

~~6TH OCT - 20TH NOV 1914~~

MAR. 1918 - MAR 1919.

FROM 8 BDE 3 CAV DIV
BOX 1156

TO HUSSARS BDE
BOX 1166

Army Form C. 2118.

WAR DIARY
or
INTELLIGENCE SUMMARY

8th Bell until 12th Mar - then 6th Bde
By 10th (P.W.O.) Royal Hussars

Vol 37

Place	Date	Hour	Summary of Events and Information	Remarks and references to Appendices
TERTRY.	March 1918 March 1st		Squadrons under their leaders.	
"	" 2nd		Squadrons under their leaders.	
"	" 3rd		C of E Church Parade in HQrs shed at 9.30 a.m.	
"	" 4th		Squadrons under their leaders.	
"	" 5th		Squadrons under their leaders.	
"	" 6th		Squadrons under their leaders.	
"	" 7th		Squadrons under their leaders.	
"	" 8th		Squadrons under their leaders.	
"	" 9th		Squadrons under their leaders. About 8 p.m. the Camp was bombed by hostile aircraft, one bomb dropping on one of pits.Huts occupied by "D" Sqdn. killing 6 O.R. and wounding 35, one of whom died after being admitted to hospital.	
"	" 10th		The L.O. inspected the Regiment less "D" Sqdn. on Sunday Order at 8.30 a.m.	
"	" 11th		Regimental drill at 8.30 a.m. and taken on strength 2/Lt G.E. Rapley arrived from Base	
"	" 12th		Squadrons under their leaders. The Regiment ceased to be attached to the 8th Cavalry Brigade and joining the 6th Cavalry Brigade	
	" 13th		The Regiment moved to the DEVISE area.	
DEVISE	" 14th		Squadrons under their leaders.	

WAR DIARY

INTELLIGENCE SUMMARY.

Army Form C. 2118.

MARCH 1918.

10th (P.W.O.) Royal Hussars

Place	Date	Hour	Summary of Events and Information	Remarks and references to Appendices
DEVISE	March 15th		The Regiment paraded mounted at 8.30am for Regimental drill. Major D.A. Lowinsky D.S.O. 19th Royal Hussars assumed temporary command of the Regiment pending arrival of their leader.	Woolfing copy
"	16th			
"	17th		G.O.C. 6th Cav. Bde inspected the horses of the Regiment in the stables at 11-30 am. & at Check Parade at 12 noon in the Barrack Sqd.	
"	18th		Regiment found working party of 7 Officers & 130 O.Rs for work in forward area. Party fell ed marched & fully armed	
"	19th		working party of 3 Off. & 130 O.Rs.	
"	20th		working party of 3 Off. & 130 O.Rs. O.C. D.A.D.C. inspected the Regimental dismounted at 4-30 pm.	
"	21st		Heavy enemy bombardment of the whole front line opposite our stand to at 4-30 am. The Regiment was ordered to stand to and moved out at 5-0 pm and marched to BEAUMONT near HAM where the Brigade bivouaced in a field. the dismounted Brigade was ordered to be formed next morning	
BEAUMONT	22nd		The dismounted Brigade left by bus early in the morning commanded by Lt. Col. Burt, 3rd Dragoon Guards. Regt. party commanded by Capts. G.H.E. Holmes M.C. with Lieuts. Gaskell, Gough, Bingley, Ralli, Field and Kellaway (See Appendix "B")	

WAR DIARY or INTELLIGENCE SUMMARY

Army Form C. 2118.

10th (P.W.O. Royal) Hussars

MARCH 1918

Place	Date	Hour	Summary of Events and Information	Remarks and references to Appendices
BEAUMONT	Mar 23rd (cont'd)		Led horses under Major Williams moved to PONTOISE near NOYON, arriving about 1-0 p.m.	
PONTOISE	" 23rd	About 10-0 a.m.	Orders were received for as many mounted men as possible to be turned out and to form in column under Brig. Gen Harman, 1 Bde, 3rd Cav. Divn. to proceed at once. 70 men were turned out. Major Williams took command of the Brigade party (about 160 strong). Lieut Lord Edwin Stroke went with Regt party (see Appendix "A") The remainder of the Regt and led horses under Capt Gaskel going moved to the afternoon to CARLEPONT and bivouacked outside the village	
CARLEPONT	" 24th		Led horses remained in bivouac	
"	" 25th		Led horses left for Ollencourt but were left at CARLEPONT under 2/Lt Ditchburn, with one horse to each man. Remainder moved to OLLENCOURT, arriving about 1-0 p.m.	
"	" 26th		Another mounted party of 50 men & 1st Lt. left under Major Lewis, Royal Dragoons. The Col M.O. & 1 N.C.O. remained & moved to CHOISY — the Regt party also proceeded from Ollencourt for CARLEPONT & should have also rejoined	
CHOISY	" 27th		Dismounted party rejoined. Led horses & 2/Lt Ditchburn's party took to them. Major Inman's party also rejoined from SEMPIGNY, having done nothing.	
"	" 28th		Another dismounted [?] 2 holds near the camp about 6-0 a.m. Lieut E.D. Tally slightly wounded	

WAR DIARY
or
INTELLIGENCE SUMMARY.
(Erase heading not required.)

Army Form C. 2118.

10th (P.W.O.) Royal Hussars

Place	Date	Hour	Summary of Events and Information	Remarks and references to Appendices
MARCH 1918				
CHOISY	Mar 29th		The Brigade moved to AIRION	
AIRION	" 30th	6.0 am	The Brigade left at 6.0 am and marched to a bivouac near SAINS-EN-AMIENOIS in support of the line South of the Somme	
SAINS-EN-AMIENOIS	" 31st		Remained in bivouac at RACINEUSE farm	

Fred H. Coty
Lt. Col.
O.C. 10th (P.W.O.) Royal Hussars

WAR DIARY or INTELLIGENCE SUMMARY

APPENDIX "A"

Army Form C. 2118.

10th (P.W.O.) Royal Hussars

MARCH 1918

Working Copy

Diary of Major A. Williams Wynn'd the Park under Brig Gen Harman

Place	Date	Hour	Summary of Events and Information
PONTOISE	Mar 23rd		The composite troop of the 10th Royal Hussars left PONTOISE and marched to BERLANCOURT. In the afternoon Lieut Drake was sent on patrol from Divisional H.Q. to report on situation at BEAUMONT-EN-BEINE and CUGNY. In the evening the Regt. was dismounted towards ESMERY-HALLON. The Regt not being required, they returned and bivouaced for the night near BERLANCOURT.
BERLANCOURT	24th		The Regt "Saddled up" at 4.0 am and moved back to a position N.W. of VILLESELVE. Early in the morning they took up a position N.W. at VILLESELVE which was held till midday when they retired to COLLEZY. In the afternoon orders were received to charge a body of Germans near the canal north of HILL 81. and of favorable to retake HILL 81. The Regt. advanced and took about 100 prisoners 3 M.G's and killed many of the enemy. The 3rd Dragoon Guards though established themselves on HILL 81. The Regt. bivouaced for the night at GUISCARD.
GUISCARD	25th		The Regt. harnessed before dawn and bivouaced at LAGNY. In the afternoon rebutted about 10am from Patrol, and to support the Infantry in party under Lord Edward Seymour. Lord Edward advanced at LAGNY. Dismounted party returned about 8 pm and the Reg'l. Bivod'd all night and found a standing patrol on SERMAIZE

APPENDIX "A" (Cont'd)
10th (P.W.O.) Royal Hussars

WAR DIARY
or
INTELLIGENCE SUMMARY

MARCH 1918

Place	Date	Hour	Summary of Events and Information	Remarks and references to Appendices
LAGNY	26	Sheet 2 60ty 1	The Regiment left before dawn and bivouaced near DIVES Should 8am they were shelled and had to move back repeatedly afterwards they were sent up to high ground N.W. of COY Spuls square kept forward to discover the situation. The Regt again moved forward and took up position at the Château in the BOIS DES ESSARTS in support of the 7th Canadian Cavalry Brigade who were holding the road from SUZOY to SCRUCOURT. About 4 p.m. the right flank on Hill 105 gave and retired. The Regiment N.W. of COY at once to form a defensive flank on high ground N.W. of COY to cover the retirement of the 7 & Canadian Brigade from BOIS-DES-ESSART'S. The Regt retired later the Enemy having taken up a new line behind, and bivouaced at ELINCOURT	
ELINCOURT	27		The Regiment marched to CHEVINCOURT in the afternoon	
CHEVINCOURT	28		The Reg. was employed in CHEVINCOURT and found patrol by day and night to keep touch with the Enemy front line	
"	29		The composite troop rejoined the Regiment at ARION	

Casualties Sustained
Major Williams (Concussion from his horse falling
1. O.R. Killed
15. " Wounded
" " Missing

Geo. Williams
Lieut 10/(P.W.O.) Royal Hussars
Adjt. 10/(P.W.O.) Royal Hussars

MARCH 1918

APPENDIX "B"

WAR DIARY
or
INTELLIGENCE SUMMARY

(Erase heading not required.)

Sheet 62 f / 10th (P.W.O.) Royal Hussars

Place	Date	Hour	Summary of Events and Information	Remarks and references to Appendices
VIRY NAUREUIL	March 22nd	5.0 a.m.	Diary of Dismounted Brigade. Ref. Map 1/100,000 The Dismounted Brigade arrived at VIRY-NAUREUIL at 5.0 a.m. and took up a position just W. of VOUEZ and dug in. The Brigade advanced on this front to Hill 130 N.E. of NAUREUIL, where it moved to a position on a line running through the W. of NAUREUIL, which was at once dug in.	
NAUREUIL	" 23rd	11.30 a.m.	At 11.30 a.m. the Germans broke through N. up to VOUEZ-ROUEZ road. The Brigade moved forward until the left on the VOUEZ-ROUEZ road to a new position. About 1.30 p.m. orders were received to retire to the road west of the NAUREUIL. This line was held about 4.30 p.m. when the left was driven in and the enemy advanced on the village. The Brigade retired to a position ½ mile S.W. of the N of NAUREUIL on W. edge of the village. The enemy hung on the village. There Capt. G. E. S. Palmer, M.C. was wounded.	
"	" 24th	8.0 p.m. 2.0 p.m.	At 2.0 p.m. the Brigade left NAUREUIL and fell back to CHAUNY via VIRY NAUREUIL, and at 6 a.m. dug in on position on the CHAUNY-JUSSY road, with the right dug in ½ mile N.E. of CHAUNY. This position was held till 8.30 a.m. when the left of the line gave way and the Brigade retired to the CHAUNY	

MARCH 1918

WAR DIARY
INTELLIGENCE SUMMARY

APPENDIX "B" (Cont'd)
Army Form C. 2118.

Sheet 2 Copy 1 10th (P.S.B.) Royal Hussars

Place	Date	Hour	Summary of Events and Information	Remarks and references to Appendices
NOUREUIL	March 24th (cont'd)		Here the Brigade dug in again and received till the order was received to fall back to ABBECOURT and take up a position behind the canal and the river. The Brigade arrived at 11.0 p.m.	Appendix C
ABBECOURT	25th		At 3.0 a.m. the Brigade moved to QUIERZY and took up positions N.E. of QUIERZY. Evert Gaskell was wounded here at 7.0 a.m. A retirement was made from this position at 10.30 a.m. and a position taken up on the high ground about LES BRUYERS.	
LES BRUYERS	26th		At 11.0 a.m. the Brigade was relieved by the French & marched back to TRACY-LE-MONT. From there horses were available, and the dismounted Brigade rejoined the horses at 2.30- 27th	

F.W.Wickham
Lt. Col.
Octg. 10th (P.S.B.) Royal Hussars

6th Cav.Bde.
3rd Cav.Div.

WAR DIARY

10th (PRINCE OF WALES'S OWN ROYAL) HUSSARS.

A P R I L

1 9 1 8

WAR DIARY or INTELLIGENCE SUMMARY

Army Form C. 2118.
10th (P.W.O.) Royal Hussars Vol 38

Place	Date	Hour	Summary of Events and Information	Remarks and references to Appendices
RACINEUSE FARM	1st April		The Brigade moved at 6.0 a.m. to GENTELLES WOOD in support of the 2nd Cavalry Division, were not employed, and moved in the evening to a small wood S. of BLANGY TRONVILLE, and about one mile N.N.W. of GENTELLES WOOD.	
GENTELLES WOOD	2nd "		The Regiment remained in bivouac.	
FOUILLOY	3rd "		The Regiment moved at 4.30 a.m. to FOUILLOY and came under the 1st Cav. Divn. as reserve. 1st Cav. Divn. were holding the line from the SOMME and through L HAMEL to WARFUSSEE ABANCOURT. They were relieved that evening by the 14th Division.	
	4th "		The enemy attacked the 14th Division at 8.0 a.m. and the Regt moved up to support towards HAMEL. The Infantry were rapidly retiring and the Regiment was soon holding a line the high ground W. of HAMEL. "D" Sqdn under Lieut Stanhard was pushed out to seize the E. end of the Bois-de-HAMEL, but came under very heavy fire, my hill and word and lost about 50 horses and were forced to fall back to the high ground W. of the Bois-de-VAIRE. The Regiment held this position all day. The 15th Australian Brigade were on our left up to the SOMME and troops over the whole of our line by nightfall. The 7th Dragoon Guards were held up to reinforce the 10th Hussars about midday. Lt.Col. H.D. Tomkinson being wounded, Lt.Col. Sparrow	Tomkinson

(App29) Wt. W12439/M1295. 73. 10.9. 1/17. D. D. & L., Ltd. Forms/C. 2118/4

WAR DIARY or INTELLIGENCE SUMMARY

Sheet 2 copy 1   10th (P.W.O.) Royal Hussars

Place	Date	Hour	Summary of Events and Information	Remarks and references to Appendices
CACHY	4th April (contd)		7th Dragoon Guards was in command of the Sector during the afternoon. Lieut. Eban Kelleroy & I still were wounded, 4 O.R's killed, 18 O.R's wounded. V.W. O.R's missing. At 9 p.m. orders were received for the Regt to rejoin the Brigade and form a dismounted party of 90 rifles like of route the S.W. end of the BOIS-de-VAIRE. The Regt. under Capt. Godby moved back to the horses which were about 1 mile E. of FOUILLOY and rode round to Brigade H.Q. about 1/2 mile N. of VILLERS BRETONNEUX. Capt. Godby remained in command of dismounted party with Lieuts. Legh, Hughes, Corbett & Robinson & took over the line on left of 3rd Dragoon Guards	
	5th		about 7am on 5th. The left Sqd. linked with the Australians W. of the BOIS-DE-VAIRE. Led horses returned to bivouac near BLANGY TRONVILLE. The dismounted Brigade was heavily shelled during the night, a few men being hurried by shell fire. The Brigade was relieved by the Italians on the evening of the 5th & returned to bivouac near BLANGY TRONVILLE, arriving about 5.am on the 6th	
BLANGY TRONVILLE	6th		The Brigade moved at 9.30.am to CAMON where all men were got under cover. Captain H.S. Phipps, Lt. Col. Campbell & H.W.G. Stirling & 98 O.R's of the W. Domin. Yeo. with 78 horses joined as reinforcements. 10 drafts of 32 O.R's from the Base also joined.	
CAMON	7th		This day was spent in reorganisation. Lt. Col. L.J.S.C. Stilwell, C.M.G., D.S.O. Essex Yeo. assumed command of the Regiment.	

WAR DIARY or INTELLIGENCE SUMMARY

Army Form C. 2118.

10th (P.W.O.) Royal Hussars

Sheet 3 copy 1

Place	Date	Hour	Summary of Events and Information	Remarks and references to Appendices
CAMON	April 8th		H.Qrs & Shakespeare N.S.Y. took over the duties of Divisional troops of 3rd Cav. Division & One 1/2 Troop who proceeded to H.D. 3rd Cav. Divn. "O" Reinforcement arrived from N.S.Y.	
"	"	9th	Bde Gen. Seymour D.S.O inspected the Regiment at 10.45 am. On the CAMON-ALLONVILLE road and is Greatly touched & "B" Echelon join't Regt. 17 O.Rs were reported as 12th Royal Dragoons & 22 O.Rs to 3rd Dragoon Guards.	
"	"	10th	Squadrons under their leaders.	
"	"	11th	The Regt. less "B" Echelon which was left at CAMON handed at 7.15 am. and marched to Brigade starting point at RIVIERY & moved via AMIENS - BERNAVILLE - AXEULE-CHATEAU to billeting area of BUIRE-AU-BOIS, where Regiment halted for the night.	
BUIRE-AU-BOIS	"	12th	About 11.30 am word was received that the Brigade was on 1/2 hrs notice to move up, and at 2.15 pm the Regt paraded and marched via WAVRANS & FLEURY to HESTRUS where it halted for the night.	
HESTRUS	"	13th	At 3.00 am word was received that the Brigade would move to BAILLEUL-LES-PERNES. Starting at 6.30 am marched via TANGRY. On arrival at BAILLEUL-AUX-PERNES the Brigade off saddled and stood to at 3 hrs notice. At 2.0 pm orders were received that X.R.H would raid the next village of RUMERVAL.	

Army Form C. 2118.

WAR DIARY
or
INTELLIGENCE SUMMARY.
(Erase heading not required.)

10th (P.W.O.) Royal Hussars

Place	Date	Hour	Summary of Events and Information	Remarks and references to Appendices
AUMERVAL	April 14th		The Regiment "stood to" saddled up, from 6.0 to 7.0 am & remained on 1½ hours notice.	
"	15th		The Regiment remained in billets and "stood to" at 3½ hours notice from 7.0 am.	
"	16th		The Regiment "stood to," saddled up, from 7.0 to 7.30 am & remained on 3½ hours notice from that time. The C.O. inspected "D" Sqdn & H.Q., in marching order at 7.45 am.	
"	17th		The Regiment "stood to"; saddled up, from 7.0 to 7.30 am & remained on 3½ hours notice. The C.O. inspected H.Q. Signallers & Signallers of "B" "C" and "D" Sqdns in barrack gardens at 7.30 am. 1st R.D. Bruce and 20 R.O.R. joined from Base Ges. "B" Echelon also rejoined.	
"	18th		The Regiment saddled up and "stood to" from 7.0 to 7.30 am and remained on 3½ hours notice. Lieut. E.F. Infield, 2.O.R. 593 riding horses joined from Base Ges.	
"	19th		The Regiment saddled up & stood to from 7.0 to 7.30 am & remained on 1½ hours notice, ready to proceed in reserve to 11th Corps, if necessary.	
"	20th		Regiment saddled up and stood to from 7.0 to 7.30 am and remained on 1½ hours notice.	

INTELLIGENCE SUMMARY.
(Erase heading not required.)

Sheet 15 copy 1   10th (P.W.O.) Royal Hussars

Place	Date	Hour	Summary of Events and Information	Remarks and references to Appendices
AUMERVAL	April 21st		The Regt "stood to" from 7.0 to 7.30 a.m. The C.O. inspected the Regt from marching order in the order "D", "C", "B" Sq'dns H.Q. Reg't on 1½ hours notice	Weeping Copy
"	22nd		Regt "stood to" from 7.0 to 7.30 a.m. Sq'dns to Riding School & Troop training Dress - drill order	
"	23rd		Regt "stood to" from 7.0 to 7.30 a.m., and remained at 3½ hours notice	
"	24		Regt "stood to" from 7.0 to 7.30 a.m. Sq'dns to Riding School and Troop Training. Major E.H.L. Selway awarded D.S.O. Lieut W.H. Gough to the E.F.C. and the "Croix de Guerre" the F.C.	
"	25th		The Regt stood to at 3½ hours notice. Troop 6.0 to 8.0 a.m. rifle they unpacked saddles & proceeded to shoot & Tg'dn training, & remained at 3½ hours notice	
"	26th		The Regt stood to at 3½ hours notice from 6.0 to 8.00 a.m. when they unpacked saddles & proceeded to shoot & Tg'dn training & came on 3½ hours notice	
"	27th		The Regt stood to at 3½ hours notice from 6.0 to 8 a.m., unpacked saddles & proceeded to shoot & Tg'dn training and came on 3½ hours notice	
"	28th		The Regt "stood to" at 8.0 a.m., off saddling after Tg'dn Leaders inspection & remained on 3½ hours notice. F.C. Service	

INTELLIGENCE SUMMARY

Sheet 6 Coty 1 10th (P.W.O.) Royal Hussars

Place	Date	Hour	Summary of Events and Information	Remarks and references to Appendices
AUMERVAL	April 28th (contd)		in the Church, AUMERVAL at 8.30am, and C of E service in the School AUMERVAL at 6.15 p.m.	
"	29th		The Regt stood to at 3¾ hours notice at 8.0am. unpacking saddles & proceeding to troop and fg'ty training. Lt. Col. Tomkinson, S.D.O. awarded bar to A.L.O. Captain G.E. Going the M.C., Lieut A.F. Lockett & Regt Sergt Major la Croix de Guerre, and Sergt Pelow & Cpl Jochen the C.B.	
"	30th		The Regt stood to at 3¾ hours notice at 8.0am. Squadrons to short exercise in the afternoon.	
"			During the time the 3rd Cav. Div. has been situated in the PERNES area, one Brigade has been detailed to move to the assistance of the XI Corps if required. Up to the 25th April, the Brigade on duty was detailed to hold the defences just E. of ST VENANT. Since that date it has been detailed to hold the bridges over the AIRE Canal E of BUSNES and a portion of a railway line just E. of BUSNES. La line STEENBECQUE - BUSNES. The 6th Cav. Bd. has taken turn and turn about with 7th Cav. Brigade, being on duty three days at a time.	

J.W. Whitmore Lt. Col.
C.O. 10th (P.W.O.) Royal Hussars

MAY 1918

WAR DIARY
or
INTELLIGENCE SUMMARY.

Army Form C. 2118.

10th (P.S.O.) Royal Hussars. Vol 39

Place	Date	Hour	Summary of Events and Information	Remarks and references to Appendices
AUMERVAL	May 1st		The Regiment stood to. Saddled up from 6.0 to 8.0 am at 3/4 hrs notice, ready to move to the assistance of XI Corps if required. & at 8.0 am. came on 3/4 hrs hours notice. The C.O. inspected the Regiment in marching order commencing at 7.0 am.	
"	2nd		Regiment stood to. Saddled up from 6.0 am to 8.0 am when they came on 3/4 hours notice, unpacked saddles and proceeded to troop and sqdn training.	
"	3rd		Regt stood to at 3/4 hrs notice from 6.0 to 8.0 am came on 3/4 hrs notice, unpacked saddles and proceeded to troop and sqdn training	
"	4th		The Regiment paraded at the Church, AUMERVAL at 8.20 am and marched to Brigade Mtg Pt. at S. end of PERNES, & from there marched via VALHOUN - ST POL - FLERS do billeting area of ROUGEFAY where Regt halted for the night. Brigade order of march BHQ, XRH, 3rd D Gds, 1st RDgns, C. Batty, 6 M.G. Sqdn etc.	
ROUGEFAY	5th		The Regiment paraded at 2.0 pm and marched to new billeting area of VILLERS L'HOPITAL, where it picketed for the night.	
VILLERS L'HOPITAL	6th		The Regiment paraded at 9.15 am and marched to Brigade Hdqrs. at MEZEROLLES, & from there marched via DOULLENS -	

WAR DIARY or INTELLIGENCE SUMMARY

Army Form C. 2118.

10th (P.o.W.O.) Royal Hussars

Place	Date	Hour	Summary of Events and Information	Remarks and references to Appendices
VILLERS L'HOPITAL	May 6th (Sun)		BEAUDESNE — TOUTENCOURT to 4nil concentration area of CONTAY, arriving about 4.0 p.m., and bivouacing in that area.	
CONTAY	"	7th	The Regiment stood to at 2 hours notice from 6.0 a.m. but did not saddle up. 1 working party of 2 subalterns and 145 O.R.'s under Capt. R.S. Phipps proceeded and fully armed, in the lines at 6.0 p.m. for work in the forward area.	
"	"	8th	The Regt. stood to at 2 hours notice from 6.0 a.m.	
"	"	9th	The Regt. saddled up & stood to ready to move off from 5.0 a.m. but at 7.30 a.m. off-saddled and came in two hours notice.	
"	"	10th	The Regt. stood to saddled up, from 5.0 to 5.30 a.m. when they off-saddled and came in 2 hours notice. 1 at 8.0 a.m. on duty hours notice. 1 working party of 3 Officers and 145 O.R.'s paraded mounted and fully armed, in the lines at 6.0 p.m. and proceeded for work in the forward area under the L.E.B.	
"	"	11th	The Regt. stood to at 1 hours notice from 5.30 a.m. and at 2 hours notice from 8.0 a.m. Lieut Lord de W. Hart awarded the Military Cross and No. 31377. Pte J.P. Hall the Distinguished Conduct Medal.	

WAR DIARY
or
INTELLIGENCE SUMMARY

Army Form C. 2118.

Sheet 3. Copy 1.   10th P.W.O. Royal Hussars

MAY 1916.

Place	Date	Hour	Summary of Events and Information	Remarks and references to Appendices
CONTAY	May 12		Regt stood to saddled up at 5.0 a.m., off saddled at 5.30 a.m. and came on 1 hours notice, and on 1½ hours notice from 8.0 a.m. Working party of 1 Officer & 9 o.r. under Capt. V.B. Gordon-Canning, M.C., paraded for work at 9 a.m., marched in marching order for work on the forward area. C.O. & R.S. Service at 8.0 a.m & 9.0 a.m	Weather
"	13		Regt stood to, saddled up from 5.0 to 5.30 a.m. when they came on 1 hour notice & off saddled & at 8.0 a.m. came on two hours notice. Working party of 2 Officers & 145 O.R. horses were being re-shod and the party marched back to bivouac on completion of task.	
"	14		Regt stood to at 5.0 a.m, but did not saddle up. At 5.30 a.m they came on 1 hour notice, and at 8.0 a.m. on 2 hours notice	
"	15		Regt stood to, saddled up from 5.0 to 5.30 a.m. off saddled and came on 1 hour notice, and on two hours notice from 8.0 a.m. Working party of 2 Officers and 100 O.R. paraded marched in the tides at 11 a.m. and proceeded for work on the forward area.	
"	16		Regt stood to saddled up from 5.0 to 5.30 a.m. when they off saddled and came on 1 hour notice from 8.0 a.m. on two hours notice	

Army Form C. 2118.

WAR DIARY
or
INTELLIGENCE=SUMMARY.

(Erase heading not required.)

Third H. Corps. 10th (P.S.O.) Royal Hussars

Place	Date	Hour	Summary of Events and Information	Remarks and references to Appendices
MAY 1918				
CONTAY	May 17th		The Bgde moved back to billeting area of BELLOY-SUR-SOMME. The Regiment paraded at 5.0 and marched to Brigade starting point at AGNICOURT, and marched via RAINNEVILLE-COISY-BERTANGLES-VAUX-EN-AMIENOIS-ST SAUVEUR to BELLOY-SUR-SOMME arriving about 11.0 am and bivouacing in the wood at the northern end of the village.	
BELLOY-SUR-SOMME	18th		The day was spent in settling in Camp and in cleaning up.	
"	19th		Brigade Church Parade at 11.0 am after which the Corps Commander Lieut-General Sir R.L. Haking K.C.B, C.V.O, S.O. inspected the Guards of the 6th B. and awarded during the recent operations.	
"	20th		Equitation and troop training from 9.15 to 10.45 am Stables. Bombing and Lewis Gun classes in the afternoon.	
"	21st		Equitation and troop training from 8.45 am to 10.15 am Lewis gun, bombing and musketry classes in the afternoon. 2/Lt. B.S.D Aldous M.C, G.H Everett and H.S. Corfield joined and Reinforcement of Camp.	
"	22nd		The day was spent in a general cleaning up.	
"	23rd		Equitation and troop training 8.45 to 10.15 am. Hot Class bombing and musketry classes in the afternoon.	

WAR DIARY
or
INTELLIGENCE SUMMARY.
(Erase heading not required.)

Army Form C. 2118.

Sheet 5 Copy 1. 10th/P.W.O. Royal Hussars

MAY 1918.

Place	Date	Hour	Summary of Events and Information	Remarks and references to Appendices
BELLOY-SUR-SOMME	May 23rd (cont'd)		from Reinforcement Camp.	
"	24th		Equitation and shoot training from 9.0.a.m. to 10.45.a.m. Lecture for Officers at 5.30.p.m. by Major James on "Cooperation between Aeroplane and Cavalry."	
"	25th		Grazing and inspection of arms and ammunition.	
"	26th		Coy E Church Services at 11.0.a.m., 12.15.p.m. and 6.0.p.m.	
"	27th	8.30.a.m. to 10.0.a.m.	Troop and Sq^{dn} training. Stables, bombing & musketry classes in the afternoon.	
"	28th	8.30.a.m. to 10.0.a.m.	Troop and Sq^{dn} training. Stables, bombing & musketry classes in the afternoon.	
"	29th	9.0.a.m. to 11.0.a.m.	Regimental Scheme.	
"	30th		Squadrons under their Leaders. Stables, bombing and musketry classes in the afternoon.	
"	31st		The Brigade moved up to the BEHENCOURT area in relief of 7th Cav. Bde. The Regiment paraded at 7.45.a.m. and marched via LA CHAUSSÉE — BERTANGLES — VILLERS BOCAGE — MOLLIENS-AU-BOIS — Regiment bivouaced in wood about ½ mile S.W. of BEHENCOURT Chateau.	

FitzCWilliam
Lt Col.
Commanding, 10th (P.W.O) Royal Hussars

WAR DIARY
INTELLIGENCE SUMMARY

Army Form C. 2118.

10th (P.W.O.) Royal Hussars

WO 39

JUNE 1918

Place	Date	Hour	Summary of Events and Information	Remarks and references to Appendices
BEHENCOURT	1st June to 13th June		The Brigade stood to each day at 1½ hours notice to move in support of III Corps if required. On 3rd June and every third day the Regiment found a working party of 3 Officers and 150 O.Rs for work on communication trenches.	
"	14th June		The Brigade was relieved by 7th Cav. Bde. and moved back to BELLOY-SUR-SOMME.	
BELLOY-SUR-SOMME	15th June to 24th June		Squadron, troop and Regimental training in mornings. Musketry, Hotchkiss classes &c. in the afternoons. 69 Refresher was carried out by the Regt. On the 22nd at which the Corps Commander, Lt. Gen Sir C.T. McM. KAVANAGH, K.C.B., C.V.O., D.S.O., was present. Owing to the large number of cases of influenza in the Brigade, it was decided to move the Brigade to another area.	
"	25th June		The Brigade moved to the SOUES area, X.R.H. being billeted at REINCOURT.	
REINCOURT	26th June to 30th June		Squadrons under their leaders &c.	

J.W. Hutchinson. Lt. Col.
10th (P.W.O.) Royal Hussars

Army Form C. 2118.

WAR DIARY
or
INTELLIGENCE SUMMARY.
(Erase heading not required.)

Sheet 1. Copy 1.   10th (P.W.O.) Royal Hussars

Place	Date	Hour	Summary of Events and Information	Remarks and references to Appendices
RINCOURT	July 1st to July 31st 1918.		General training was carried out during month, particular attention being paid to musketry, Intelligence and scouting under Lieut. J. Robinson, M.C. Captain D.S. Phipps, M.C., N.S.Y. was struck off the strength on 11th July on being absorbed into establishment of Res. Corps Tactical School. 2/Lieut. C. de C. Mullins joined Regt on 10th July. Captain the Earl of Airlie, M.C. rejoined from England and 42 reinforcements arrived from Base on 30th July, and were taken on the strength.	

A.D. Wotherwe
Lt. Col,
Commanding 10th (P.W.O.) Royal Hussars.

WAR DIARY or INTELLIGENCE SUMMARY.

Army Form C. 2118.

10th (P.W.O.) Royal Hussars

Place	Date	Hour	Summary of Events and Information	Remarks and references to Appendices
AUGUST 1918.				
RIENCOURT	1st to 5th Aug.		Mounted training and musketry.	
"	6th Aug.		The Regt left RIENCOURT at 10.40 h. and marched to Bde concentration area about PONT DE METZ, X R H being billeted at RENANCOURT and arriving there about 3.0.a.m. 7th	
RENANCOURT	7th	"	Left RENANCOURT at 9.0 P.m. and moved up to an assembly area about 2 miles East of LONGEAU.	
"	8th	"	The attack on the German line opposite AMIENS started from DETNANGOURT on the North to the river LUCE on the South, the front being on the outskirts of the British line, the Australian Corps was on the left and the Canadian Corps on the right of the British line. The Cavalry Corps was behind the Canadians to exploit their success. The attack commenced at 4.20.a.m. and the infantry advanced straight to their objectives without much opposition. The Canadian Cavalry Brigade was leading the Brigade and were first up the Brigade to come in contact with the enemy. The 3rd Can. Bde operated on the left. The 6th Bde. In Reserve Brigade & followed via CACHY. DEMUIN 9 N. of BEAUCOURT. Towards evening the Regt was ordered to support the	Rolling Map 10th R. Hussars

WAR DIARY or INTELLIGENCE SUMMARY

Army Form C. 2118.

(Erase heading not required.)

10th (P.W.O.) Royal Hussars

AUGUST 1918

Place	Date	Hour	Summary of Events and Information	Remarks and references to Appendices
	8th Aug (Cont'd)		7th Brigade to the South of CAIX to a point about 1 mile N.E. of LE QUESNEL. The Infantry held a line opposite to the front of this. "D" Sqdn had 2 troops at the head of the main valley supporting south of CAIX and 1 troop of "B" Sqdn with Hotchkiss & Machine Guns. The remainder of the Regt was held on hand about the middle of the valley. At this time Capt Gordon Canning was commanding the Regt, Col Whymore having taken over the Brigade from Brig Gen Seymour who had had to leave owing to illness. Major G.A. Gosling was away on Liaison duties.	10/8 killed 11/0 R & sd
	9th Aug		During the day & early morning the Regt suffered some casualties from shellfire. Lieut H. Howlett was killed & Lieut H.F. Robinson wounded. Some 70 horses were lost. Some by shellfire & others by breaking away during the shelling. During 9th Aug the Regt moved back to [?] west of CAIX where the Division was withdrawn to Corps Reserve.	[illegible marginal notes]
CAIX	10th Aug		The Brigade moved at 5.30 p.m. & followed up the Infantry so as to avoid their advance. It was believed that the Cav: Bgd in this who moved back through the 3rd on the way up, 6th Brigade was to operate on the	

WAR DIARY
or
INTELLIGENCE SUMMARY.
(Erase heading not required.)

Army Form C. 2118.

AUGUST 1918   Sheet 3 Copy 1

Place	Date	Hour	Summary of Events and Information	Remarks and references to Appendices
CAIX	10 Aug (cont'd)		night & the 1st Cav. Bde. on the left. The Brigade moved off via BEAUFORT to FOLIES. On arrival there the situation in PARVILLERS and the high ground between DAMERY and ANDECHY was occupied by the enemy. The 3rd Dragoon Gds advanced via BOUCHOIR & the Road by POUVROY, trying to get to the country beyond occupied by our armoured cars. At once the 9.6 Battles advance for mounted troops became practically impossible. The Canadian Cavalry Brigade tried to take Pt 100 between DAMERY and ANDECHY and 10th Hussars were ordered to support them if they succeeded, but owing to not being able to get off the main ROYE road they came under very heavy machine gun fire and were unable to go get at Pt 100. 6th Cav. Bde. then concentrated at FOLIES for the night.	
FOLIES	11 Aug		The 3rd Cav. Bri. was not moved and about 5.30 p.m marched back to the BOVES area, the 6th Cav. Bde. billeting at FOUENCAMPS	
FOUENCAMPS	12 Aug to 14 Aug		Squadrons under their Leaders	

AUGUST 1918

WAR DIARY
or
INTELLIGENCE SUMMARY

10th (P.W.O.) Royal [Hussars?]

Place	Date	Hour	Summary of Events and Information	Remarks and references to Appendices
FOUENCAMPS	15th Aug		The Brigade moved back to the LE MESGE area, X.R.H being billeted at RIENCOURT.	
RIENCOURT	16th Aug		Squadrons under their leaders	
"	17th Aug		Mounted drawing of Hotchkiss Rifles, and	
"	20th Aug		drawing of spare kits	
"	22nd Aug		The Regt stood to at 3 hours notice, and at 10 pm orders were received to the effect that the Brigade would move to the FIEFFES area. The Regt paraded and moved to Rue TPBS at 11.3.5pm. "B" Echelon moved to BETTENCOURT ST OUEN	
FIEFFES	23rd Aug 24th Aug		The Regt stood to at 3 hours notice	
"	25th Aug		The Brigade moved to area of WILLENCOURT, X.R.H being billeted at VITZ VILLEROY.	
VITZ VILLEROY	26th Aug		The Brigade moved to area of NUNCQ, X.R.H 9/R Royal Dragoons being billeted at SIBIVILLE.	
"	27th Aug 28th Aug		Brigade on 3 hours notice.	

WAR DIARY
or
INTELLIGENCE SUMMARY.

Army Form C. 2118.

10th (P.W.O.) Royal Hussars

AUGUST 1918

Sheet 5 Copy 1

Place	Date	Hour	Summary of Events and Information	Remarks and references to Appendices
SIBIVILLE	29th Aug		Regt. still on 2½ hours notice. Billeting party ordered to proceed to WAILLY (3½ miles S.W. of ARRAS) at 3.0 p.m. Cancelled at 4.30 p.m. Motor cyclist sent to bring party back.	
"	30th Aug		Regt. with A1, A2 Echelon & 1 Section 6 M.G.Sqdn. left for WAILLY at 7.0 p.m.	Leading troop
WAILLY	31st Aug		Regt. reviewed at WAILLY. All roads in the area BEAURAINS - TILLOY - WANCOURT - BOIRY - BECQUERELLE reconnoitred. Regt. came under orders of Canadian Corps and Col. B.J. Litmore attached to H.Q. Canadian Corps H.Q. with reference to the modified plan of operation.	

J. W. Graham Lt. Col.
Cdg. 10th (P.W.O.) Royal Hussars

WAR DIARY
or
INTELLIGENCE SUMMARY

Army Form C. 2118.
VOL 43

10th (P.W.O.) Royal Hussars.

SEPTEMBER 1918.

Place	Date	Hour	Summary of Events and Information	Remarks and references to Appendices
WAILLY	1st Sept 18		The Regt came under the command of Brig. Gen. R. Bushell, C.M.G., D.S.O., who had been given command of the Canadian Independent Force. This force was sub-divided into 3 Groups. Lt. Col. A. H. C. Kenilmore, C.M.G., D.S.O., in command of the Regt.'s Group. The composition of this Group was :- 10th Royal Hussars, Canadian Lt R.L. Horse (less 1½ Sect.), Canadian Field Artillery, 6 Heavy Armoured Cars, 2 Light Armoured Cars and 12 motor cycles for inter-communication. This Leading Group concentrated about 2 miles N.W. of WANCOURT about midday 1st Sept.	Moving up
WANCOURT	2nd		The Regt led the vanguard with "D" Sqn (under Capt the Earl of Airlie) in front with the armoured cars. Advance was at ST ROHARTS factory (N.W. of VIS-EN-ARTOIS) at ZERO hour (5.0.am). The Infantry halted their third objective, a line along the ridge from West of CAGNICOURT to East of RIOT at 8.30.am, and the leading Group advanced. The armoured cars were able to reach the Infantry line but could get no further owing to Artillery at A.G. fire. Likewise "D" Sqn could not get beyond cross roads ARRAS. CAMBRAI and HENDICOURT-DURY roads. Several reserves were placed but owing to enemy M.G. fire we could make no further advance, and at 5.30. p.m. were ordered to return to WAILLY.	
WAILLY	3rd		Regiment remained on 2 hours notice.	

Army Form C. 2118.

WAR DIARY
or
INTELLIGENCE SUMMARY.
(Erase heading not required.)

SEPTEMBER 1918.

Sheet 2. Copy 1.   10th (P.W.O.) Royal Hussars

Instructions regarding War Diaries and Intelligence Summaries are contained in F.S. Regs., Part II. and the Staff Manual respectively. Title pages will be prepared in manuscript.

Place	Date	Hour	Summary of Events and Information	Remarks and references to Appendices
WAILLY	4th Sept		Regt. arrived on 2 hours notice. Received that the Regt. would rejoin 6th Cav. Bde. the next morning.	
"	5th	"	The Regt. returned to SIBIVILLE and B' Echelon rejoined.	
SIBIVILLE	6th	"	The Brigade moved to WAIL area, and marched via BLANGERVILLE - LINZEUX - WILLEMAN. X.R.H. were billeted at VIEIL HESDIN.	
VIEIL HESDIN	7th	"	Squadrons under their leaders. Regt. on 2 hours notice.	
"	8th	"	C of E Service in the School at 6.30.p.m. Lieut. W.S. Thesiger rejoined Regt. from leave.	
"	9th to 15th Sept	"	Squadrons under their leaders. Grazing &c.	
"	16th	"	The Brigade concentrated in the GRIGNY area for Cavalry Corps manoeuvres on the 17th. The Regt. was billeted at GRIGNY.	
GRIGNY	17th	"	The Regt. took part in Cav. Corps Scheme attended by the Commander in Chief.	
			Scheme. - Our Infantry had broken through on the line BLANGY - ST POL. Cavalry Corps was launched in pursuit.	
				1st Cav. Div.

Army Form C. 2118.

WAR DIARY
or
INTELLIGENCE SUMMARY.
(Erase heading not required.)

10th (P.W.O.) Royal Hussars

Instructions regarding War Diaries and Intelligence Summaries are contained in F.S. Regs., Part II. and the Staff Manual respectively. Title pages will be prepared in manuscript.

SEPTEMBER 1918

Place	Date	Hour	Summary of Events and Information	Remarks and references to Appendices
	17th Sept (Contd)		1st Cav. Div. were leading Division and had orders to seize and hold crossings over the river AUTHIE between GENNE - NERGNY and WAVANS. 3rd Cav. Bde. as soon as this was done were to push through and seize the high ground BERNAVILLE and BEAUMETZ, and destroy the Railway Junction at CANDAS. 6th Cav. Bde. as left Bde of the Division and 10th Hussars were Reserve Regt. 16th (Q.L.) under Capt. Hurlock were posted at 1.30 h.y. from BOIRE - AU - BOIS as flank guard to the Brigade which was advancing on a route MAIZECOURT - PROUVILLE. The (Q.L.) were opposed by M.G's in BEAUCOURT which were overcome. Gene Jire then rounded. The Regt billeted for the night at BOISBERQUES.	
BOISBERQUES	18th Sept		The Regt returned to VIEIL HESDIN.	
VIEIL HESDIN	19th "		The Brigade moved to the PREVENT area, X.R.H. being billeted at LIGNY-SUR-CANCHE.	
LIGNY-SUR-CANCHE	20th & 21st Sept		Squadrons under their Leaders, X.R.H. Cav. Corps Royal Carp. on 21st. O. Rejoined from Church Service at 9 P.m. in the School	3. 10th Hussars
"	22nd "			
"	23rd "		Stout above was carried out by R. B. & Sqdns in the neighbourhood	1st Cav. Bde.....

SEPTEMBER 1918

Army Form C. 2118.

WAR DIARY
or
INTELLIGENCE SUMMARY.
(Erase heading not required.)

Sheet H Copy 1   10th (P.W.O.) Royal Hussars

Place	Date	Hour	Summary of Events and Information	Remarks and references to Appendices
LIGNY-SUR-CANCHE	24th (Sept)		The Regt took part in a Brigade inter-communication scheme.	Signed Copy
"	25th	"	The Brigade moved to an area COUIN - LOUVENCOURT, X.R.H. billeting at the former place.	
"	26th	"	The Brigade moved to an area about FRICOURT - MEAULTE. X.R.H. bivouacing in open S. of CO in DERNACOURT.	
MEAULTE	27th	"	The Brigade moved to an area about 1 mile N.E. of HEM.	
HEM	28th	"	Brigade remained in bivouac.	
"	29th	"	About 1.30 p.m. orders were received that the Brigade would move forward. Bde halted & bivouaced at VERMAND.	
"	30th	"	Remained in bivouac.	

2.10.18.

T.W. Whitmore Lt. Col.,
Cdg. 10th (P.W.O.) Royal Hussars.

OCTOBER 1918

WAR DIARY
or
INTELLIGENCE SUMMARY

Army Form C. 2118.

Sheet: Copy 1

10th (P.W.O.) Royal Hussars

Place	Date	Hour	Summary of Events and Information	Remarks and references to Appendices
BIHECOURT	1st Oct		The Regiment remained in bivouac.	
"	2nd "		The Brigade moved up to an assembly area near BELLENGUISE, leaving bivouac at 08.00. The 4th of the 3rd Cav. Div. was to exploit any success of the 4th Army who were attacking. However at 10.30. orders were received to return to BIHECOURT	
"	3rd "		At 10.30 the Brigade moved up again to BELLENGUISE, from there to an assembly area S.W. of JONCOURT, which was reached at 15.00. 3rd Dragoon Guards attempted to advance towards RAMICOURT via PRESELLES, but no advance could be made and the Brigade returned to bivouac about PONTRU.	
PONTRU	4th "		The Regiment remained in bivouac all day.	
"	5th "		The Brigade moved back to TREFCON, and the Regt was billeted to stables and huts used in winter 1917-1918 by the Royal Horse Guards.	
TREFCON	6th "		Remained in Camp.	
"	7th "		"	
TREFCON	8th "		The Brigade moved up to an assembly area about	

OCTOBER 1918.

Army Form C. 2118.

WAR DIARY
or
INTELLIGENCE SUMMARY.

Placed 2 Copy 1 10th (P.W.O.) Royal Hussars

Place	Date	Hour	Summary of Events and Information	Remarks and references to Appendices
	8th Oct (cont'd)		MAGNY-LA-FOSSE, leaving Camp at 04.45. The role of the 3rd Cav Div was to follow the 1st Cav Div in exploiting the success of the 3rd & 4th Armies attacking in the direction CAUDRY-BOHAIN. The 6th Cav Bde was in Corps Reserve. At about 09.00 the Brigade moved up to just N. of WIANCOURT, and returned to LIGNY-LE-FOSSE for the night.	
LIGNY LE FOSSE	9th Oct		The Brigade moved at 05.00 to an assembly area E. of PONCHAUX. The role of the 3rd Cav Div was to keep close touch with the Infantry, and at the opportunity occurred, to push through and to exploit any high ground W. & S.W. of LE CATEAU. The 6th Cav Bde followed along the line of the main ESTREES - LE CATEAU road, to a position S. of MARETZ. C. Sqdn. acted as flank guard to the Division. At 13.00 orders were received that if the Infantry took HONNECHY, the Canadian Cavalry Brigade would advance via HONNECHY MAUROIS on the Divisional objective, and the 6th Cav Bde would advance (south of HONNECHY) Brigade (South of HONNECHY) Brigade advanced. The 1st Royal Dragoons on REUMONT, and the 3rd Dragoon Guards to the E. outskirts of HONNECHY. The 10th Hussars followed the 3rd Dragoon Guards. Heavy M.G. fire was met with from the direction of ESCAUFOURT, as the Regt advanced round the South of	A.M. allowance front money

OCTOBER 1918.

Army Form C. 2118.

WAR DIARY
or
INTELLIGENCE SUMMARY.

(Erase heading not required.)

10th (P.W.O.) Royal Hussars

Cavalry Corps — Cavalry.

Place	Date	Hour	Summary of Events and Information	Remarks and references to Appendices

REUMONT — 9th Oct / HONNECHY — Another attack on the line REUMONT - HONNECHY was now made and the Regiment bivouaced for the night between REUMONT and MAUROIS, and the outpost line was taken over by the XIII Corps by dusk. The Regiment suffered casualties as follows:- Captains D.J. Harland and Lord J.C. Powell, Lieuts. I.M. Palli, Waugh & I.P. McKie, Lieut. J.E. Drake M.C., Lieuts. T.& O.Rs. wounded, & 7 O.Rs. killed. 30 O.Rs. wounded, & 106 horses. The casualties were mostly caused by shells and aeroplane bombs.

REUMONT / 10th / The Brigade was concentrated by 06.00 in the valley S. of TROISVILLES, and remained in that area all day. Little progress was made by the Infantry beyond the line W. and S. of NEUVILLY - W. outskirts of LE CATEAU. The Regiment bivouaced for the night just N.E. of MONTIGNY.

MONTIGNY / 11th " / The Brigade moved at 13.30 to ELINCOURT, where it halted.

ELINCOURT / 12th " / Remained in billets.

" / 13th " / The Brigade moved West to area of BANTEUX on the HINDENBURG Line, where it halted for the night.

OCTOBER 1918   Army Form C. 2118.

WAR DIARY or INTELLIGENCE SUMMARY.
(Erase heading not required.)

10th (P.W.O.) Royal Hussars

Place	Date	Hour	Summary of Events and Information	Remarks and references to Appendices
BANTEUX	11th Oct.		The Brigade moved West to area of ETRICOURT-MANANCOURT. X.R.H. being billeted in huts &c. in the latter place.	
MANANCOURT	15th Oct.		Squadrons under their leaders.	
"	21st "		Captain S.L.G.W. Earl of Airlie, M.C. struck off strength on being invalided to England on 7.10.18.	
"	22nd "		The Regiment took part in a Brigade scheme.	
"	23rd "		Squadrons under their leaders.	
"	24th "			
"	25th "		The Commanding Officer inspected the Regiment, less transport & cyclists, in Fighting Order. Awarded the Military Cross. Lieut. F.R. Jenwyn.	
"	26th "		The Commanding Officer inspected the transports & cyclists in marching order.	
"	27th "		C. of E. Evening Service in the Canteen at 18.00.	
"	28th "		The Regiment participated in a Brigade scheme.	
"	29th "		Squadrons under their leaders.	
"	30th "		Squadrons under their leaders. The G.O.C. 6th Cav. Bde. inspected "A" Tp., 1 Troop in marching order, 1 Troop in drill order, 1 Troop with stripped saddles, & 1 Troop in watering order.	

OCTOBER 1918

WAR DIARY
or
INTELLIGENCE SUMMARY.

Army Form C. 2118.

(Erase heading not required.) 10th (P.W.O.) Royal Hussars

Sheet 5. Copy 1.

Place	Date	Hour	Summary of Events and Information	Remarks and references to Appendices
MANANCOURT	31st Oct		Squadrons under their leaders.	

Frowsilians
Lieut-Col.
Commanding, 10th (P.W.O.) Royal Hussars.

NOVEMBER 1918.

WAR DIARY
or
INTELLIGENCE SUMMARY.

(Erase heading not required.)

Army Form C. 2118.

10 (P.W.O) Royal Hussars

Vol 47

C.A.Williams Lt.

Place	Date	Hour	Summary of Events and Information
MANANCOURT	Nov. 1st		Squadrons under their leaders.
"	2nd		The Regiment participated in a Brigade Scheme.
"	3rd		C. of E. Holy Communion at 10.00 am the Canteen Shed.
"	4th		Squadrons under their leaders.
"	5th		Squadrons under their leaders. About 14.00 hours orders were received that the Brigade was on three hours notice to move up.
"	6th		The Brigade moved North to MARQUION where it halted for the night.
MARQUION	" 7th		The Brigade moved South via AUBIGNY-AU-BAC - DOUAI to ESQUERCHIN where it halted for the night.
ESQUERCHIN	" 8th		The Brigade moved East to area of FRETIN where the Regiment was billeted.
FRETIN	" 9th		Squadrons under their leaders.
"	10th		The Brigade moved East, via TOURNAI, to area of GOUTRAIN - RAMECROIX, where it halted for the night

NOVEMBER 1918

WAR DIARY or INTELLIGENCE SUMMARY
Army Form C. 2118.

10th P.W.O. Royal Hussars

Place	Date	Hour	Summary of Events and Information	Remarks and references to Appendices
GOURAIN	11th Nov		The general idea was that the 6 Cav. Bde. was to push on ahead of the Infantry and get as its final objective for the day ENGHIEN-SOIGNIES. 10th Royal Hussars were leading Regiment. 1 X.R.H. and 3rd R.G.ds in support. Two troops 1st patrols 2 of H.Q.'s were sent ahead of the Brigade as attacking patrols with instructions to keep ahead of the leading Regiment and gain touch with the enemy. The Regiment reached LEUZE at 10.30 and gbn.l.10.35. The following from Cavalry Corps was received. "Hostilities will cease at 11.00 today; 11.11.18. Troops will stand fast on the line established, and reported to Corps H.Q. Line of outposts will be established and reported to Corps H.Q. No Rearguards or troops will be collected organised ready to meet any advance. There will be no military fraternising with the enemy. Further instructions will be issued." (Sgd) G. REYNOLDS, Major. Cav. Corps. 08.10. It was arranged that as 11.00 all trumpeters were to sound the "Cease fire" The 1st Hussars on LEUZE-LEUZE the Regt & 3rd R.G.ds [?] signals Royal O Hussars 2 [?] but an Infantry Battn came up quickly from the [?] had. There were also sounded by [?] the Regt at 11.00. The trumpeters sounded "Cease fire" & the Band played the National Anthems of the Allies. The ceremony terminated by the Mayor of the town making a speech about the Allies. The Regiment moved out to the E exit of LEUZE and [?] [?]	

A.L. Hammond, Lt

WAR DIARY
INTELLIGENCE SUMMARY

10th (P.W.O.) ROYAL HUSSARS.

NOVEMBER, 1918. SHEET 3. COPY 1.

Place	Date	Hour	Summary of Events and Information	Remarks and references to Appendices
GOURAIN	11th (cont'd)		Here until a message came by aeroplane stating that Regiments were to move back to last night's billets. The Regiment arrived there about 18.00 hours. The two troops on patrol moved so quickly that great difficulty was experienced in recalling them after "Cease fire" had sounded at 11.00 hours. 2/Lt. KYTE's troop got within ½ mile of BASILLY and at 12.30 were fired on by a light gun, mounted on a motor lorry, at the cross roads beside the Y in BASILLY. Two M.G: fired from the Western edge of the BOIS DE SILLY. This patrol rejoined the Regiment at 20.00. The patrol under Lieut. LOCKETT did not get in touch with the enemy and rejoined the Regiment at 08.00 the following morning.	OAKillers 2
WILLAUPUIS	12th		The Brigade moved to an area BERTINCROIX, WILLAUPUIS, WASMES, PONTENCHÉ, the 10th Hussars being billeted at WILLAUPUIS.	
	13th, 14th, 15th, 16th		Squadrons under their Leaders.	
			The Commanding Officer inspected the Regiment in Marching Order. Squadrons under their Leaders.	
St. MARCOULE	17th		The Brigade marched East via LEUZE - ATH - GHISLENGHIEN to an area about CROISETTE where it halted for the night, 10th Hussars being billets at ST. MARCOULE. 1st R.Dns. were on right of 10th Hussars, 3 D.G.s on left, 10th Hussars with Brigade Group in support. "C" Squadron were attached to Cavalry Corps as escort to Corps Commander.	
SAINTES	18th		The Brigade moved East via ENGHIEN to SAINTES where the Brigade Group was billeted. Cordial reception from the civilian population who turned out with bands, flags &c.	

NOVEMBER 1918.

WAR DIARY
of
INTELLIGENCE SUMMARY.

10th (P.W.O.) ROYAL HUSSARS.

Place	Date	Hour	Summary of Events and Information	Remarks and references to Appendices
SAINTES	19th & 20th		Squadrons under their leaders.	
LIMAL	21st		The Brigade moved to OTTIGNIES area, 10th Hussars being billeted at LIMAL. The Brigade passed over the field of WATERLOO.	
TAVIERS	22nd		The Brigade moved via PERNEZ to area about EGNEZEE, HQ 10th Hussars being billeted in TAVIERS, A Squadron at NEPTINNE and B Squadron at BOLINNE.	
	23rd		Squadrons under their leaders. Major E.H.N. WILLIAMS, D.S.O., rejoined the Regiment from Cavalry Corps School, DIEPPE.	
ST GERMAIN	24th		The Regiment paraded at 11.30 and marched to billeting area of ST GERMAIN – LIERNU.	
	25th – 30th		Squadrons under their leaders.	

Trouton[?]
Lieut.Colonel.
Commdg. 10th (P.W.O.) Royal Hussars.

WAR DIARY

10th (P.W.O.) ROYAL HUSSARS

INTELLIGENCE SUMMARY

DECEMBER 1918.

Army Form C. 2118.

Book No 1. Sheet 1.

Place	Date	Hour	Summary of Events and Information	Remarks and references to Appendices
ST. GERMAIN.	1st	—	C. of E. Service at UPIGNY at 18.30.	
	2nd–4th	—	Squadrons under their Leaders.	
	5th	—	The A.D.V.S. inspected the horses of the Regiment.	
	6th & 7th	—	Squadrons under their Leaders.	
	8th	—	C. of E. Service in the School at 09.30.	
	9th	—	Squadrons under their Leaders.	
MOHA.	10th	—	The Brigade moved to new billeting area, 10th Hussars billeting at MOHA.	
	11th	—	Squadrons under their Leaders.	
SERAING-LE-CHATEAU.	12th	—	The Regiment moved to winter area SERAING-LE-CHATEAU and "A" & "B" Squadrons at VERLAINE, Headquarters being at SERAING-LE-CHATEAU.	
	13th–15th	—	Squadrons under their Leaders.	
	16th	—	Squadrons under their Leaders. Courses of instruction in connection with the Army Educational Training Scheme commenced.	
	17th–24th	—	Squadrons under their Leaders.	
	25th	—	Christmas Day was spent in the usual English style. A dance was held at VERLAINE in the evening, to which the civilian population were invited.	
	26th–31st	—	Squadrons under their Leaders.	

W. Wickham
Major,
Commanding 10th (P.W.O.) Royal Hussars.

WAR DIARY

Army Form C. 2118.

10th (P.W.O.) Royal Hussars

JANUARY 1919

Instructions regarding War Diaries and Intelligence Summaries are contained in F. S. Regs., Part II. and the Staff Manual respectively. Title pages will be prepared in manuscript.

Place	Date	Hour	Summary of Events and Information	Remarks and references to Appendices
SERRING LES CHATEAU	1st to 31st Jan 1919		The Regiment, less "C" Sqdn, remained in Billets at VERTRAINE and SERRING-LES-CHATEAU. "C" Sqdn. remained attached to Cavalry Corps Headqrs, SPA, as Escort Squadron to the Corps Commander. During the month Lt. West, 2/Lt. Sherbert, 2/Lt. H.H. Brown, 2/Lt. Kelly, 2/Lt. 6. Knight, 2/Lt. H. Daigh and 165 O.R. proceeded to U.K. for demobilisation &c, and all horses in the Regiment were classified for demobilisation. Lieut. B. V. Taylor was rejoined in England for duty with the Reserve Regiment on 15th Jan 1919 and Lieut. S.V. Lockett was invalided to U.K. on same date. The Regimental Band joined Regiment from England on 13th Jan 1919.	

F.H.Wilson Lt. Col.
Cmdg. 10th (P.W.O.) Royal Hussars

FEBRUARY 1919

Army Form C. 2118.

WAR DIARY

INTELLIGENCE SUMMARY

10th (P.W.O.) Royal Hussars

Place	Date	Hour	Summary of Events and Information	Remarks and references to Appendices
SERAING	1st		The Regiment less "C" Sqdn. remained in billets at VERVAINE and SERAING-LE-CHATEAU. "C" Sqdn. remained attached to Cavalry Corps Headqrs. SPA, as Escort to Sqdn. to the Corps Commander.	50
LE CHATEAU	28th Feb 1919		During the month 98 O.R. were demobilised and about 236 horses were despatched to Animal Embarking Depôts &c. 60 of which were for Cavalry having purposes in England. 2/Lt R.V. Gaston and 2/Lt D. Strangham joined Regiment on 17th & 18th Feby respectively. Lieut. H.O. Morrison was evacuated to England on 15th February 1919.	

First Wilson Lt-Col.
Cdg. 10th (P.W.O.) Royal Hussars.

No 51

Confidential

WAR DIARY.
of
10th HUSSARS.
March 1919

WAR DIARY

INTELLIGENCE SUMMARY

Army Form C. 2118.

MARCH 1919

10th (P.W.O.) Royal Hussars

Place	Date	Hour	Summary of Events and Information	Remarks and references to Appendices
SERAING LE CHATEAU	1st to 13th March 1919		The Regiment less "C" Sqdn. remained in billets at SERAING LE CHATEAU and VERLAINE. "C" Sqdn. remained attached to Cavalry Corps H.Q. SPA as Escort Sqdn. to Corps Commander. Following Officers joined :- 2/Lt. O.B. CHURCH, 6th March. 2/Lt. E.R. KIMBELL, 14th Hussars, 7th March, 2/Lt. B.G. BEARMAN, 14th Hussars, 10th March. 2/Lt. A.D. Hillhouse proceeded for demobilization on 8th March. 61 Riding horses were taken over from 3rd D.G's on 1st March.	
	14th March		Regiment commenced march to GERMANY to join 1st Cavalry Division, and to form part of the Army of Occupation. Regiment less "C" Sqdn. paraded at 09.30 hrs, and marched to SPRIMONT. 73 O.R's of 15th Hussars joined in the morning to assist in the move. Capt A.W. Phipps, M.C, Lieut P.R. Kenyon, M.C., 2/Lt J.B. Lees and 59 O.R's of the Regt. were left behind to be demobilized.	

Army Form C. 2118.

WAR DIARY
or
INTELLIGENCE SUMMARY.
(Erase heading not required.)

10th (P.W.O.) Royal Hussars

SHEET 2. Copy 1.

Place	Date	Hour	Summary of Events and Information	Remarks and references to Appendices
SERAING LE CHATEAU	14th (Cont.)		Headqrs. billeted at SPRIMONT, "A" Sqdn at DAMRE & "B" Sqdn at LINCE.	
SPRIMONT	15th		Regiment remained in SPRIMONT area.	
"	16th		Regiment remained in SPRIMONT area. Following details joined the Regt. 7/1st R.W. Horse, 34 O.R's from 4th Hussars. 72/1st Batt and 52 O.R's from 20th Hussars. 409 Horses joined from 4th Hussars.	
"	17th		Regiment (less "C" Sqdn) paraded at 10.00 hrs and marched to THEUX.	
THEUX	18th		Regiment (less "C" Sqdn) paraded at 09.30 hrs & marched to RAEREN. "C" Sqdn rejoined Regt, marching independently & billeting at NISPERT.	
RAEREN	19th		Regiment paraded at 10.00 hrs and marched to HONGEN. "A" Sqdn billeted at HONGEN, "B" Sqdn at WARDEN and "C" Sqdn at HEHLRATH.	
HONGEN	20th		Regiment paraded at 10.00 hrs & marched to final area, previously occupied by 19th Hussars. Headquarters, "A" & "B" Sqdns billeted at KONIGSHOVEN, and "C" Sqdn at MORKEN. Regt. now became part of 9th Cav. Bde & administered by 1st Cav. Div.	

Army Form C. 2118.

MARCH 1919

Instructions regarding War Diaries and Intelligence
Summaries are contained in F. S. Regs., Part II.
and the Staff Manual respectively. Title pages
will be prepared in manuscript.

WAR DIARY
INTELLIGENCE SUMMARY.
(Erase heading not required.)

SHEET 3 Copy 1

10th (PWO) Royal Hussars

Place	Date	Hour	Summary of Events and Information	Remarks and references to Appendices
KONIGSHOVEN	21st to 31st March 1919		Regiment remained in billets in KONIGSHOVEN and MORKEN. The 73 O.R's of 15th Hussars were returned to their Unit, and horses surplus to establishment were disposed of to other Units. Capt A.W. Phipps & 51 O.R's of the party left at SERAING LE CHATEAU proceeded for demobilization on 16th March. Lieut P.P. Janzy, 2/Lt J.B. Lees & the remainder of O.R's proceeded on 22nd March. Lieut E.H. Parr & 40 Returnable O.R's of 11th Hussars joined Regt. from 12th Royal Lancers on 29th March. Capt E.W.G. Plowes M.C. & Hon Capt W.H. Druce 2/Lieut C. de L. Mullens proceeded for demobilization on 28th March & Lieut E.H. Parr, 11th Hussars on 30th March. Lt Col J.H.D.G. Whitmore C.M.G., D.S.O., proceeded on leave to U.K. on 29th March and Major E.H.W. Williams D.S.O. took over command of the Regiment.	

Weymann Major
Cdg. 10th (PWO) Royal Hussars

www.ingramcontent.com/pod-product-compliance
Lightning Source LLC
Chambersburg PA
CBHW081245170426
43191CB00037B/2051